Everything So Seriously

Everything So Seriously

Douglas Treem

The New York Quarterly Foundation, Inc.
New York, New York

NYQ Books™ is an imprint of The New York Quarterly Foundation, Inc.

The New York Quarterly Foundation, Inc.
P. O. Box 2015
Old Chelsea Station
New York, NY 10113

www.nyqbooks.org

First Edition

Set in New Baskerville

Layout and Design by Raymond P. Hammond

Library of Congress Control Number: 2010938049

ISBN: 978-1-935520-14-6

Everything So Seriously

Acknowledgments

The following poems first appeared in *New York Quarterly*, some in slightly different forms, and are reproduced here by permission: "Babe Ruth"; "Carole's Boyfriend"; "David Janssen"; "Dennis Wilson"; "Did You Ever Hear Him Sing 'Young and Beautiful'?"; "My Sick Teacher"; "The Ribcage"; "The Starch."

Contents

for Jane

Everything So Seriously

The Ribcage

His skin was cocoa
brown and there was
writing going down
the right side of his
ribs. Tattoos on dark
people are hard to
read, so I asked him
if it was Chinese.
No. Japanese.
And what does it
mean?
It's a prayer, he
told me.
It asks that after
I die I be made
into a god.
Yes, I said to him.
It's best to make
out a will.
Although he didn't get
my joke he smiled at
me.
Beautifully, I'm forced to say.
He had a beautiful smile.
I don't have a beautiful
smile, so I keep the
door locked on my face
as a public service.
Sometimes people
who think themselves
kind will tell me
to smile.
Smile. Smile, they

demand, confident that
they mean well.
So I smile at them.
Like taking a command
on a witness stand.
Don't smile, they say.
Stop smiling, please.
They walk off
shook from hands
to heart.
Unsmiling back at
him, I asked, The
god of what?
The question kicked
his plug out.
I could see he hadn't
thought of that, and
that suddenly the
enduring of a Japanese
scroll
being etched onto him
was called into question
as to its value, given
the ghastly backfires
that could lie in the sacred texts
of others of another
tongue.
He beheld the unknown
and it froze him.
He held a skate-
board upside down
on his shoulder.
Maybe that, I said, and

tapped the board
to snap him to.
He looked at his
skateboard as if
he'd just noticed
it there and now
wondered what
it was for.
Then the implanted
vision I suggested
hit him in all its
typical religious
glory and the smile
returned to reclaim
his face for beauty
and faith. The god
of skateboarding
could not then resist
flying away from me
on one leg
outstretched and
arched, embracing the
eternity of
joy that he had
requested skintight
and painfully down
along his side.
The god of piddling
rue watched him.
The god of missing
by a mile. The god
of crying over spilt
milk, the god of

low-grade fever
and chipped teeth,
the god of lost library
books, the
god of the wincing smile
that is an apology
for not being able
to smile.

The Mystery Guest

The private blitz
I heard it called
by a man who would fall
in that war inside him.
He would be bombed and
strafed to defeat
by a microscopic army
that invaded through his veins.
But not before he told me
a war story.
The Battle of the Epiphany.
No machine guns.
No parachutes.
Just three library books
one day away from being
overdue
in arms that looked like pipe cleaners
splattered with purple.
Three hardcovers
that might as well have been
manhole covers
were brought back
to the Epiphany.
His branch. On time.
It was the long march
the death march and
the slowest Charge of the Light Brigade
ever made.
But penalization was the enemy
and he was willing to die
in the effort to deny punishment
any further gain
in the war

of his one world.
Epiphany means the end of
the journey.

It was in that time
in the first half of the eighties
I visited Eddie.
Eddie of Tony and Eddie.
Tony of Tony and Eddie
told me that soon it would
be
Tony. No Eddie.
He was in Beth Israel
on the ward for it.
Two rows of beds in a long
room that dissolved
into the light of huge windows at
the end.
Eddie stared straight at me.
"Who's there?" he said.
I was invisible now. Everything
was, to Eddie.
"Hi, Eddie," I said.
In puzzlement he took
a wild guess at who I was.
He was wrong.
"No," I said, "but whoever that
is I'm sure he's a nice guy
with a deep voice."
Then he guessed me.
And that wasn't bad. Two
guesses. Considering we were
only neighbors, and in New York

that's not much.
"How are you doing, Eddie?"
Eddie smiled and nodded and
stared in my direction.
Then I flashed on something.
What Eddie said.
As if he had smelled or
heard or felt it.
"I just thought of something," I
said.
"When I was a kid. A little kid.
'What's My Line?' was on TV on
Sunday nights."
"What's My Line?" said the man in the
bed next to Eddie's. He rolled on
his side toward us.
"Soupy Sales," he said. He was
a young man down to his last
layer of skin. His voice had
the Spanish lilt.
"No," I said. "That was the new one.
I mean the old one."
"There was an old 'What's My
Line?'" The young man seemed
amazed.
There was much before his time.
There would be little of it.
"That's Luis," Eddie said.
"Hola, Luis," I said. "There was an old
'What's My Line?' The original.
It had Arlene Francis.
Dorothy Kilgallen.
And Bennett Cerf. And it came

from New York City.
The last contestant on the show
was always a celebrity.
So the panelists would all
wear masks. And try to guess
who it was. When the
celebrity would come on they
would sign their name
on a chalkboard and the
audience would recognize
them and just go crazy.
Screaming and whistling and
cheering. Just go berserk
at the sight of them. The
one I remember best was
Ingemar Johansson."
"Who?" said Eddie and Luis.
"What, are you guys owls?"
I said.
"He was the heavyweight
champion of the world
for a little while.
Anyway, I used to think:
When I grow up
I'll go to New York City.
I'll be the celebrity guest
on 'What's My Line?'
Well, when I came in
and you didn't know who it
was.
That made me think of it.
I guess this is as close
as I'm ever gonna get

to it."
"You want to do it again?" Eddie
asked me.
"We could do it a little better,"
he said.
"Why not? O.K.," I said.
"I'll be the audience," Luis
volunteered.
I got up. I went out and
I came back in.
Luis did not let me down.
He gave me a downright ovation.
Whistling, too.
In other beds some men
stirred, but none awoke.
I sat down.
Eddie made a mask of his
hands over his eyes.
"Are you in the entertainment
industry?" he asked.
"No," I said, high-voiced to
disguise myself.
That so tickled Luis that
he gave me some genuine
applause.
"Are you a sports figure?"
"No."
"Are you involved in politics?"
"No."
Eddie's tongue stuck out
to help him think.
It was white.
"Are you a furniture mover?"

21

"Yes," I said
in my own true voice.
"Did you help me and Tony
carry a couch all the way
up six flights of stairs?"
"Yes."
"Is it—"
He dramatically paused.
"Doug?"
"Yes."
Eddie lowered his blindfold
and clapped with it.
Along came Luis.
"What brings you to town,
Doug?" asked Eddie, pretending
to see me.
"Just to come on this show,
Eddie.
Like I always wanted to."
I stretched out my arms
to grasp the size of my
mock achievement.
"Who says dreams don't
come true?" I intoned on
the gallows that I visited.
"Not me," voted my skeletal
audience of Luis.
And Eddie lay back
lying in state
doing the new dance craze
that had swept New York:
The Pietà.
He draped himself across

the embrace of the
Mother of Beauty
and spoke in a voice
tender and sad itself
so as to comfort one disappointed.
"Everything comes true," he
said.
Beaming.
Blind.
Seeing nothing in that room.
He closed his eyes and
didn't die then.

Babe Ruth

From a kid on up
I went alone
And I grew a heart
Like a broken bone
That heals askew
So it always aches
Every beat it gives
A beat it takes
It never stopped
Until I slept
And no one knew
The break it kept

The Baby

I feel so sorry
for those who think
that they are me.
There are a half-dozen or so
of hard-core cases
of which one or two
will make the news
every now and then.
The saddest is the lady in Trenton
the black lady
who swears to the world
that both her sex and race
were changed
to hide her away.
I pray for that poor soul
who says that she is me.
They press their cases
and they are laughed out of court
never to be given
the one chance needed
to present the irrefutable evidence
of the shape of their skulls
or to show the mysterious
photograph
that dropped from a shelf
in an attic
that shows a child
that could only be them
surrounded by unidentifiable
adult males
in sinister poses
one a double for
if not actually

Al Capone.
Or may they simply be allowed
to swear on the Bible
and tell of the dream
that comes with each night
where they are raised
from their beds
limp in the clutch
of a darker power
in the darkness of the nursery
that carries them out the
window
to the cold night air
and begins a descent
down a ladder
that never ends
that never reaches the ground.
No lawyer will take their money.
They have all
at one time or another
been arrested
for trespassing.
I had expected to be myself
and had accepted that
consequence.
But that didn't happen.
Something else happened.
I made my pilgrimage
with the intention of making it
only once.
I will make my claim,
I vowed
and claim no more

than I am myself.
The gates of the compound
were wide open.
Not a guard in sight.
The driveway
looked more like a highway
and I began the long walk
to the house in the distance
where the family lived.
I had my proof with me
on the new white shirt
I had bought that morning.
Pinned over my heart
the same way it first
had been
when I was a child
unconscious
half-dead from a dosing of
chloroform
and set down on the front
steps
of a church in Baltimore
near enough to dawn
to be found still alive.
With a piece of brown paper
torn from a grocery bag
that had two words
written on it
in pencil
that had been kept
for thirty years
in the center
of a Bible

then sent to me
along with a letter
from a deathbed.
I had been tracked down
through the Navy and the V.A.
Sister Mary Agnes
my kindergarten teacher
told me in her last written
words
that it was true.
"I cannot go to my God
with this secret on my soul.
Men came looking for you.
Not good men.
We hid you away.
Told them you were dead.
They didn't believe us.
But they went away.
We named you after our church
and the street it was on.
Paul Washington.
We obeyed the laws of God.
But you must know the truth
of who you are.
It is written
on this scrap of paper
that was pinned on the blanket
we found you wrapped in.
I go now
free
to see the face
of my Lord."
The good book had preserved it

well.
I wore it now
standing on the porch
of that big house in Hawaii.
There can be no sturdier
vessel of truth in this world
than that of a dying nun.
I believed her every last word.
I rang the bell.
No answer.
I heard it echo through the
house.
I gave the door
some hard knocks
that settled into silence.
Had I come from one abandoned
place to another?
I cupped my hands
on the windows and looked
through them.
I saw beautiful large
red chairs.
A fireplace.
A staircase that looked
like marble.
It crossed my mind
to go inside.
But I said no
I'm not a criminal
just a distant relative
dropping by.
I sat on the steps
of the porch.

Unpinned the note.
Set it down
and carefully wrote
on the back of it
my name, address, and phone number.
That was when it began.
The quiet of the day
changed.
It dropped to total
complete silence.
The birds shut off.
The breeze stopped.
The woods surrounding the house
stood stock-still.
Not a leaf fell.
Nor a bristle moved.
If a pin had been allowed
to drop I would have heard
it.
But that was not allowed.
The living world was being
held like a breath.
The only sound on earth
was my heartbeat
that sounded like the way
I had knocked
on the door.
A light began
from beneath the trees.
It grew and rose
steadily
until it had filled
the woods with itself.

Like the rising of
a buried sun.
I was surrounded by it.
And it began to move
toward me
like the closing in
of walls made
of white light
with an intensifying
warmth
that felt of fire
that set upon me
like one layer after another
of heated skin.
It seemed that nature
had risen up from its
origin
to banish a degree of coldness
to extinguish a gradation
of darkness
forever
from my life.
I knew it could dissolve me
if it wished.
But it had been sent
for other chores
reaching even unto
the knots around the bottom
of my spine.
The cemetery of dead nerves.
The battlefield of scar tissue
left from the torpedo-loading
accident

that retired me early.
Melted by the fire
of the light.
The power that encircled me
could perform the most failed
of all earthly desires.
It could undo
what had been done.
I pinned the note
to the door
my side facing out
the other side
telling its story.
My story and the lady in Trenton's
and the handful
of other men
all the same age
in two words.
"Lindbergh Baby."
As I walked back
through the light
it had begun
to lose itself
to the air.
And as I passed the gates
I heard the breeze behind me
begin to move again.
The birds were back
and a plane passed
overhead.
I wish I could tell
the people who think
they are me

just what happened
out there in Hawaii.
It would probably make them
feel a lot better about
their own evidence
and let them have the chance
to see someone else
as the nut.
They need help
and I can't help them.
But maybe some comfort
could apply
if I told them:
What you want
I have got.
If you can take it
it's yours.
I would give it to you
if I could.
I don't need it.

The Saint

In certain scrawled circles
of hell on earth
he was well known.
My bartender Pat
pointed him out.
Primly sunken was how he sat
on the edge of one of our
leather booths
at the darkest corner
of our already pretty damn dark
gay bar.
I cupped my good ear to Pat.
The bartender poured the story in.
That guy there, Pat said.
He invented the twelve-step hustle.
It sounded like a dance, I thought.
It wasn't a dance.
That cat there, man, said Pat.
He worked every A.A. room in this city.
And that's a lot of rooms.
And he burned them down, every one,
to the ground.
A young gay guy can't go to A.A. now
without everybody freezing
and sniffing for a scam.
He stank it up for good.
Pat's tale unfolded meanly
yet with that elevation that we build
into the gallows.
The man Pat told me of
sat uncommonly still
for one still alive.
He allowed himself no more

than the slightest edge of the booth
on which to perch his ass
clenching a balance
like a bird in a freezing cold.
His head bowed, his hands
clasped on his
knees.
He looked like a mourner
at a service
for someone
he had killed.
Crumpled into and frozen in
a pose of shame
like the low slump
of a bad dog.
Still as a statue called
The Penitent.
Darkly dressed, he blended
thoroughly with the darkest
part of our dark gay bar
on a night in the early
nineteen eighties
when the days for such as those
in that bar
were themselves dark.
I didn't notice him leave.

The next to last time
I saw him
was our deadest time.
A Saturday afternoon.
He was our only customer
and he wasn't buying anything.

Once again Pat filled me in.
"I told him there was no food
allowed. And he didn't buy a drink."
He was in the same dark spot.
But this time burrowed farther
into the booth.
And there was indeed food on the
table before him.
And that was not allowed.
And he had not bought a drink
which in any bar on earth
is punishable by...
well
I'm sure that there are some places
where the punishment
is death
with no worry
about questions asked.
Here I booted you out.
And any sass back
got belted.
That was the job.
I looked from Pat to him.
Sorrow.
I held it down like bile.
To see anyone that afraid.
To know that someone felt that way
when they saw me.
It made a sorrowful bond
that
unlike my trusty fear
I could not convert
to anger.

Still I began the ramrod straight
slow stately walk
that my dance master
Charles Bronson
had instructed me in.
I loomed over him with my palms
on the table
in order to pump out
my deltoids
to show an offender
just how hard I was willing
to be on myself.
I said
There is no food allowed in this bar.
As for my voice
some black guys at another job I once had
used to call me Barry Black.
Because
Barry White is black
they said.
But Barry Black is white.
The twelve-step hustler did a swoon
of sorrow.
He rocked and whined
like a creature bred on
regular punishment.
And he said
I'm sorry. I didn't know.
Now I knew my line.
At this point I was to say
Well, my bartender tells me
that he told you.
Are you calling him a liar?

That once said, the ball
was properly rolling and
all that would be left
would be my last line.
I will give you the opportunity
to walk out that door.
But I couldn't say it.
At that moment I did not want
to be paid in this world
for frightening a fuck-up
in a fucking gay bar
in New York City
dead center in the 1980s
when the clientele and the help
were dying at a steady clip.
Occasionally right before
my very eyes.
I wanted to walk out
that door myself.
He had a burger in front of him
wrapped in yellow paper.
Burger King was two doors down.
Well, finish it up I said
and don't let it happen again.
I walked behind the bar
drew a beer
brought it over to him
and set it at the table.
Then I got the refill list
from Pat who was in shock
and went downstairs
to where we kept the bottles.
I was thinking that

if I do the opposite
of everything
I always do
that direction will lead away
from the drenching pity that I felt
for my poor alcoholic bartender
the twelve-step hustler
and the bouncer that they
promoted to manager
because they couldn't afford
to have both.

We had a big night
that night.
One of the last.
I remember that several times
I had to thin the registers and
take money downstairs.
I was in my spot
around the corner
at the end of the bar
when he appeared.
I was leaning on the entry part
that opens up and down.
I leaned into it even deeper
and regarded him from over my
shoulder.
I got my first good look at him.
Instantly I thought Poe.
The portrait.
The same cracked bewildered
expression and those eyes about to
cry.

With his suit jacket. Gold
buttons. Sweater vest and tie.
I could see he was working the schoolboy
look.
Pat had told me that
Little-boy-lost had been his lure.
I want to thank you for what you
did for me he said.
He had to lean to my lean.
I tossed
That's okay at him and
looked away.
He leaned in closer and
that was too close.
He tottered precariously
nearly tip-toe and
I was preparing
to punch him
directly over his heart.
For I thought now
I was being hustled.
Did this face that launched
a thousand cashmere sweaters
and once got him his
very own car
succeed in casting
its wicked spell
on even the heart
of the straightest arrow
to ever fall in this town?
Bartender Pat once said
he would take it as
a personal offense

if anyone thought a man
as dull as me
were gay.
But did that not matter at all
to the twelve-step hustler?
Did he simply
like the squid
possess a blinding potion
he could squirt
on any poor soul
that swam by his game?
The moment he mentions money
I thought
I will become the revenge
of every older gentleman
who had wept at the sight
of the phone bill
he had stuck them with.
I unwound to face him.
Like the clank of a steel visor
down came my mean face.
We were quite close.
He had found a tightrope
in the floor
on which he balanced.
He bent dangerously closer.
He said
I have decency within me.
It was a confession.
An admittance.
It told the world not to worry.
His comeuppance
his just desert

was assured.
He was someone who knew
that people knew
all about him.
But they didn't know that.
That thing he told me.
This time I watched him leave.

The third and last time
I saw him
was in my very own neck
of the woods
Twenty-third and Third
where I watched him cross the street.
He wasn't walking really.
He was making a delicate soft
plod.
Too slow to successfully survive
crossing any street in this world
let alone in New York
though he looked as if he had just
successfully survived execution
by hanging.
His chin was on his chest.
His shoulders had rounded
themselves off.
Draped in a grey overcoat
that might have been another color
once.
He inched his way forward
carrying a black suitcase
that I sensed had to be
empty.

The cars just stopped and waited.
No one seeing him
bothered to honk.
The automatic big city adjustment
for a derelict nut?
Or the ancient instinctive recognition
of a holy man?
Like the way passing monks
can stop a battle in mid-pitch.
A pause descended upon his surrounds.
Thank God I saw his face
serene and crinkling
the surety of his joy
for knowing just where he was going
with the knowledge of the pace
required.
The foundation of his beauty had returned
exposed
like a temple found
under the rubble
of a sin city.
I wanted to follow him.
I knew I couldn't.
I might as well have tried
to imitate a butterfly
in flight.
He had gone to that place
inside him where
decency dwelt alone and inviolate.
When he got there he closed
the door behind him.
There was one last stop.
He became my saint.

What I had always wished
I had seen
an apostle
in the first year of A.D.
A walking vulnerability.
A man turned inside out
so totally
as to achieve a supreme
invincibility.
Nail him, burn him, decorate him
with arrows
he would remain beyond
the clutches
of this world.
Later when I tried to
write it down
I invented a vision for myself.
I claimed to have seen
poles of beautiful golden light
spearing through him
circular and grinding
dissolving him
erasing him gloriously.
I cited the burning ray
of a magnifying glass when
focusing the sunlight
likening it to the gaze of
God
when it picks one of us out
for a glance of grace.
But I didn't want to lie.
I didn't need to.
I didn't want to make things up.

I didn't need to.
I didn't want to craft it into poetry.
I didn't need to.
He was a saint.
St. Decency.
The patron saint of all
who don't know how good they are
who hate themselves and seek
what they think they deserve.
St. Decency went to where
he was harmless
incapable of the thought
of doing wrong.
Where he did live
in the way that makes you die
in this world.
Where I still live.
Where I pray
to him.
I wished that we had shaken hands.
We didn't.

Let me now cross
barefoot
the rocky terrain
that Mr. Tillich charted
and called
"Necessary Doubt."
What if that wasn't
the last time I see him?
What if I see him
one more time
at the exact same place

where I saw him last?
Only this time my Paul
changed his name back to Saul.
Got his old job back.
With a promotion to boot.
Alighting from a block-long limo
decked out in duds as emblematic
as the swastika in its evil.
Expensive clothes.
Pausing to receive the only thing left he seeks.
The submitting envy of the passer-by.
As I happen to pass by.
He spews a stream of smoke at me
a poison that I know will spare him
out of professional courtesy.
I am sprayed with disdain
as I lock eyes
with my enemy
whom I am commanded to love
even more than my saint.
The soul that has shattered itself
for the sake of becoming
its own vicious shards.
What would I do then?
Well, I would rewrite this poem.
It would all then be fiction.
Something I dreamed up.
But at least then
I could bring back
those great churning poles
of golden light.
I would need them
fast and bad.

Carole's Boyfriend

There was this place where we would go. Between the shows usually, but sometimes after.

You could crash there if you really had to. But mostly we would just drop by in the afternoon, get high, drink a beer. The boom box would be thumping disco. Disco was the music then, always kicking at us.

The TV would be on with the sound off. It was more a lamp than a TV. The windows were covered over with newspapers. Me and Carole would go over after the first show of the day, the twelve noon show. The Businessman's Lunch, it was called. We would usually wake up whoever had done the last show of the day before, the Nighthawk, at 2 A.M.

The newspapers were stuck over the windows with Scotch tape. The sun would light them up, and I could read the headlines about the bad shit that happened in New York City.

Mattresses on the floor. A garbage can from the street. Chairs that wobbled. A sunken couch. Thrown-away stuff that was dragged back to the place where we threw ourselves away between the shows where we fucked onstage at the Roxy.

Carole always brought her towel, a big one with Chiquita Banana on it, and she would always take a shower in that place's bathroom. Sometimes twice a day. She was a good girl.

I saw that right off when I met her. She was being beaten by her boyfriend, Scotty, in a doorway on 8th Avenue.

I had seen Scotty around. White guys take notice of the same down there and keep a respectful distance. Hey, man. Hey, man. That's it.

I grabbed Scotty by the hair. He had long blond hair just like a surfer dude. Tall skinny guy, looked like an eaten chicken. I pulled off a wig. Scotty had a line of staples on the top of his head, bridging a poorly healing wound on the top of him.

You want me to open that up for you, boy? I asked him. Take a look inside. Take a piss in it, maybe. I moved in with Carole that night and I got Scotty's job, too, which he wasn't hardly showing up for anymore anyhow.

Carole never put him down. He used to be just like you, she'd say to me. He got turned into someone else when he was roller-skating one way and a car was coming the other, and as they passed a motherfucker popped halfway out the back window and broke a golf club across the top of that kid's head. Till then he had been just like me, Carole told me.

I never did know whose place it was, or who taped up those papers on the windows.

There was this one guy who was almost always there, sitting in a big, broken lounge chair that slumped with him in front of the silent TV. A black guy with his hair straightened and frozen into a cut like the early Beatles.

I heard him called by a lot of different names, and he answered to them all. I always knew when he was high. His slump would get as frozen as his hair. And his stone indifference turned to stoned affection. The warmth of the heroin spread out of him to embrace the whole world of that room.

Buddy, he said to me, if I had your complexion I would be whispering in the president's ear. Man, he said, I went to college for free because I could run. Run like a motherfucker.

Once he made a fist and shook it gently, like he was holding something small and valuable.

If there's a God, he said then, we're all fucked. Eventually.

If there ain't, then—he opened his hand to reveal nothing— then we are all fucked here and now. I like you, he said to me. You're a good listener.

One day he asked if I would do him a favor. Carole couldn't take no shower that day, he said, because there was a dead Japanese man naked in the tub that he was hacking off pieces of, and would I be so kind as to take a piece with me when I left and dispose of it at least a mile away from here. That would be twenty blocks. Sure, I said.

He went into the bathroom. I looked at the newspapers lit up by the sun. They were from the week before. Pictures of fireworks and the tall ships. The Bicentennial had been last week. He came back holding a plastic supermarket bag, pinching the handles like he was holding the tail of a dead thing with a tail.

I reached out and took it by the lump at the bottom of the bag. I held it and felt through the plastic with my hands.

It was a hand chopped off just above the bone that sticks up at the wrist. It struck me as too small. Let me see this guy, I said.

He waved toward the bathroom but looked at the newspapers on the windows.

In the bathroom there was a man in the bathtub. A small man with one foot that had a black sock on it. The other foot was gone. One arm was gone just below the shoulder. The other arm ended just above the wrist. His head was twisted away from me, facing the bathroom wall as if he couldn't stand to look at anyone who'd come in there.

Some Jap guy, said the man, whose name, I found out later, happened to be Ronald. Angel took some. So did Candy, he said. Angel and Candy fucked at the Roxy too. I figure everyone takes some, said the guy I had heard called Duke, Prince, Miles, Shane, and Boss Shannon, the man who really can. And pretty soon it's all gone, he said.

There was a machete lying by the tub, dark with a gleaming edge.

Carole's coming over with some food, I told him. Don't let her in. Tell her I told you to tell her to meet me back at our room. Don't let her in here at all, I said, looking right at him. He shrugged to say, ain't no big thing.

I took off with the bag closed by my fist. By 42nd and 5th Ave. my damn hand hurt so much from squeezing too hard that I just wanted to have done with it.

There was a half-full trash can right there. Toss it right in and it will get buried and buried and buried again. But first and last I had to see it.

I tucked the bag under my chin and looked down. The hand was curled and reaching up at me. I closed the bag and took a look around.

The first thing I saw, that I saw everywhere, it seemed, was people holding hands.

I never noticed that before.

It looked to me like just about everyone in the world was holding someone's hand.

I stood there with a plastic bag that held a hand.

I opened the bag, reached in, and touched the hand. It was cold and the fingers were stiff. I put my thumb across the palm and wrapped my fingers over the knuckles and held it that way.

I walked up 5th Ave., my hand in the bag.

At the 79th St. entrance I went into Central Park. I went to the middle where they play ball and sat there on a bench.

51

I had the bag on my lap with my hand in it.

This may be as close as I get.

I thought that.

This may be as close as I get.

So make the most, I thought.

This might be as close as you get.

I stayed there till it started getting dark.

That was a while.

David Janssen

Good driver. Bad driver.
What does that matter?
You're going to be killed by
Somebody else. Somebody else.
I don't know who.
What matters is the car.
Your car.
You have to have the best car
You can have.
I have the best car in the world.

My mother brought me to Clark Gable.
My mother worked in the costume
Department of a movie studio.
I was seven.
She dressed me in a suit
Of herringbone twill
With a cashmere car coat
And brown felt hat.
She held my shoulders from behind
And walked me to the man.
He sat at a round card table
In the blazing total light
Of a movie set.
What movie I don't know.
Only that it wasn't you know
What.
My mother said "This is my son David.
He wants to be a movie star."
The king looked like a lion
Waking up from a happy dream
Where he had seen himself sleeping.
"Well, let's see what the cards say,"

Said Clark Gable.
With one hand he picked up
A deck of cards before him
And shuffled them with
That one hand.
With a flick of the wrist
Like the jump of a cobra
He fanned them out
Face down.
"Pick a card, son."
One card in the exact
Middle
Stuck out slightly askew.
There went my little hand.
I showed Clark Gable
The ace of spades.
"Wrong card, son. Wrong card,"
The king whispered to me.
"That one is mine."
The king tucked the card
Into his truly beautiful vest.
Dark red with fine gold stripes.
I haunted the MGM auction
Desperate to find it
And buy it.
Any price. Any price.

I won't fuck the widows of dead men
I liked or admired.
I will, however, kiss their pussies.
Not oral sex.
Not eating them out.
Kissing.

Tenderly, softly.
A little touch of the tongue
Now and then.
Like the first kiss of lovers
Who will be married.
Where was I when Kennedy was
Shot?
I was fucking one of his Hollywood
Girls.
We had the radio on.
I froze and, moving only my ass,
I took back my cock,
Kissed her pussy,
And went to the Polo Lounge to drink.
It's often been suggested
I'm a queer.
That I'm a queer and
I don't know it.
I have never fucked a man.
Never kissed one.
But I have kissed the pussies
Of the women who fucked
Men I knew.
With my lips I kissed
The lips their cocks
Had fucked.
Ordinary widows, I fuck them.
The wives of the living,
I fuck them.
John Wayne said to me
Janssen, you have fucked more women
Than J.F.K.

I had more time.
Even when he was alive
I had more time.
Now, today, maybe I have today
And tonight.
Tomorrow is an awful long
Ways away.
I have a good doctor I don't have to
Make an appointment with.
I just drop in.
He gives me five years or
Any minute now.
The heart.
It goes crazy.
Does a drum roll.
Once, twice a year.
Now every day.
I carry my nitro right next to
My cigarettes.
Pills to wake up. Booze to go to sleep.
Pills to wake you up while you are awake.
Good pills.
I haven't gained a pound in twenty years.
Unless I force-feed myself
I lose ten in one day.
So I drive by Ciro's every afternoon.
I call them first from the phone
In my car.
I drive around back by the garbage.
Always the same Mexican kid
Drops a rare steak
On my passenger seat
Through the open car window

And takes a fifty from my hand
And says thank you in Spanish.
Though we should call it Mexican
If it's said by a Mexican
Like you should call what I say
American.
I unwrap the tin foil
And eat with my fingers.
I grab it and bite off a chunk
While I drive.
There's this ex-nurse, an actress
Who lives in the Valley.
She sells drugs and hooks
A bit on the side.
A contact advised me
She's out to blackmail me.
God bless her, that cunt.
It makes me so hard.
I'll screw her and screw her
In Sandy Koufax's motel.
The one he used to own
With the big baseball on top.
Maybe I'll die there
The way my doctor describes.
My heart will go crazy
And speed up its beats.
It will cram in so many
It will skip to the end
And stop there, all finished.
I'll hear a whore singing
In the shower.
The grinding purr of the air conditioner
Will race its coolness against

The chill of my corpse
And I'll see myself
In the smoked-glass mirrors
There above the bed
Where the new owners put them
When they took over.
How long ago was that?

Poem on the Repatriation of the Remains of Battling Siki from New York to Senegal

Battling Siki
If you can
Rest in peace
In your native land

Sleep and dream
The happy times
Forget this world and
All its crimes

At the spot
Where you died
A prayer was said
A white man cried

For you
Battling Siki

Dennis Wilson

Off a road
Between Nebraska and Iowa
I was making the movie
That did not make me
A movie star.
I sat on a car
To get my picture took.
I peeled off my shirt and I got
The giggles.
I looked off sideways at the sunset
Coming down round and flattening
On the ground
Till it made me a little blind.
The man with the camera said:
Perfect light. One more. Thank you.
I closed my eyes and heard him
Walk away from the dirt to the highway.
A breeze crossed me.
It felt cool and great over my sweat.
I thought about God and I bet
That this was his touch and the sun
Was his eye and the moon
Was the other one.
Darkness was rolling out
From the sun.
These things were falling
Into place inside me.
I opened my eyes in the dusk
And I thought
I am the wick of a candle
And he has breathed the flame
Off me.
Now gone out I am alive

At last.
I foresaw my own ironic death
And shook my head and smiled
Then glimpsed little kids
On a beach
Under the roar of an airplane
With their arms out behind them
Pretending to fly.
They called my name.
They told me it was time.
I sprang off the hood.
I stuck my head in my T-shirt.
I wiped my eyes inside it.
Then I pulled it down
Over me.

Did You Ever Hear Him Sing "Young and Beautiful"?

He was standing in the rain
That's why I stopped
To ask him if he needed a ride
Much obliged, he said
As he ducked his head
And seemed to bring the storm inside
I asked where you headed
He shrugged and said
Don't know myself
Some place you could call Heaven
Or Hell
I said this here's a long road
We're both alone
I believe you have a story to tell
He said Sir, I've had no breakfast today
Nor supper the night before
But I'm feeding on the love of God
I've no need to ask for more
You see he freed me many nights ago
From this world's awful yokes
Now I roam his creation
In calm desolation
To mention him to folks.

We drove for a while
Just over a mile
The rain made me peek at the road
I said for such a young man
I can't understand
How you carry this terrible load
For the good news is bad
To those of us had

By the powers that fashion this world
It reminds us of sin
The plight that we're in
And the judgment to which we'll be
Hurled
He said I know what you mean
I've already seen
The fate that awaits most of us
I lived it all out
And sheltered by doubt
Went quietly
Without too much fuss
But the Lord threw me back
Like a fish that's too small
And told me to do it again
This time get it right
In what's left of the light
Go be the friend of a friend.

I said Do you know who you look like
I faked some delight
Yes he said with compassion
Sensing my fright
It's who I am he said
And exactly what I'm not
You see it takes a mighty big twist
To become a part of this plot
I said I heard you were dead
My laugh wasn't real
He said that part's half true
Now this here's the deal
My body died out
But my soul wasn't in

So when this world up and goes
I'll die once again
Till then I just walk
And ride now and then
To tender regards
From a friend of a friend.

I knew it was nuts
And I knew it was true
I said I got some of your records
He said most do
I didn't dare say his name
Or his nickname
Or my own
He said I ruled a gold world
Where each handle was pearled
And I died of tears shed
From the bone
I said you look mighty fit
He said I'm frozen in it
I'm at the moment before things
Went bad
So I guess I'm nineteen
Unknown to the mean
Bewildered by the poor and the sad
Because below and above
No one's lost to love
Though it sure as hell can feel
That way
You are an object of need
Like the air that you breathe
To the God
That is raining today.

He pointed off right
It was the time of near night
When light and dark
Mix into grey
I stopped the car there
He let in the air
And closed the door
Softly, I'd say.

I've tried telling some people
Who just stared at me
The things that the dead king had said
But I'd see them get scared
So's not to make them afeared
I'd pretend I was joking
Instead
So I keep my trap shut
And hide in the rut
Of birth, existence, and death
But I tell it somehow
And I say it plain now
We are each of us God's holy
Breath
With my hands on a bed
I lower my head
And I pray
With the pain in my knees
I have a friend
Who is a friend of a friend
A man who said thank you
And
Please.

My Sick Teacher

He stands at dawn
burning on the inside,
coughing stuff up.
He walks from the bed halfway to the bathroom
like crossing a river on stones.
He must inspect what he has coughed up
to check it for its color and consistency.
If it's dark and thick
if it's still dark and thick
then he will still be very sick.
He can't seem to find enough stones.
Avoid the cliche, he taught me.
Dodge it, duck it, kill it at all costs.
Okay: so he is pale as night.
Custer, he says.
Custer, he did not crack.
He holds a finger straight up.
He jerks once and half of each cell in his body flinches.
But Keats,
he says.
Keats, he says again.
The finger draws an arc in the air,
points straight down a moment,
then loses its strength and curls.
He says Keats cracked.
Standing there pale as the night,
trembling like anything other than a leaf can tremble,
he composes: Keats cracked, but Custer laughed.
For posterity, he looks at me.
He speaks with finality.
Keats cracked.
Custer laughed.

I note the revision with one nod of my head.
Suddenly he finds the stones to the bathroom
where he holds his hand to his face
to see what he coughed up.

The Lyle Alzado Workout Tape

Welcome to the other end
Of all that you valued.
Where men have no value and
You are most unwelcome.
Here the world is made
Of wet paper bags.
You could close your hand
After efforts all morning.
You can't make it a fist.
Eating is weightlifting.
Any three steps up or down
Are the three falls to Golgotha
The place of skulls.
Like the pattern of death's heads
On the black scarf
You wore knotted over
Your bare head
For the final interview
That I read
In *Sports Illustrated*
Years ago. When you were living and dying.
There you confessed to the black magic.
The steroids. The drugs.
How you would have eaten beating hearts
Ripped out of tigers
By your bare hands
To be stronger.
Fiercer. More man.
More beast. A locomotive
Spouting blood. Dreaming that
Your dick's a flamethrower.
I wish you'd told us all
To go to hell

With our gloating pity.
I wish you had attacked
Like one last snap out of
A rabid basset hound
Which you kind of resembled.
Face sunken. Eyes swollen.
Weighing less than I can bench.
But you didn't. You regretted.
You said you didn't want anyone
Else to die the way you were.
You were forty-two years
Of age. You wished for health.
I wish I were a little bigger.
In the arms, you know, Lyle.
More peak.
God rest you, Lyle Alzado.
And God give me strength.
I love your workout tape.
How you yell at me
To do what you do.
It has taught me
Painful things to do.
I bought it for two dollars
And seventeen cents
At a store that was going
Out of business.
Two seventeen is the number
On the door of the building
Where I live.
I will do
What I am told.

The Starch

Most people are going to just give up.
More than most. Almost all.
The pain will bust a big, pouring
Vein of disappointment
That will deflate them like
A doll filled with air
Sliced by a double-edged
Spanish knife.
I say that to pay tribute
To the knife I bought
At the private
Gun and knife show
That went on after
The official gun and knife show.
The seller gleaned me so quickly
That I heard his teeth click.
He spoke an invocation.
"Fascist. Officer-issue only.
Nineteen thirty-six"
As he raised it up and down
Across his palm
To demonstrate the secret
Weight
Of the thin black blade
That had collected a dark density
From its drenching in blood.
Sold.
I swear you could say they die
Of sadness while being
Beaten to death.
Saw a woman go that way.
She was curled up at first
But finally just stretched out

On her belly and buried her face
In the crook of her elbow
Like she was trying to sleep
In a room filled with light
While the two men killing her
Just kept stomping down
Like they were trying to flatten
Cans.
She was a whore who may have given
Them the clap. Or else she stole.
That part was never clear.
Dead, she looked like
Someone who had cried
Herself to death.
Some poor girl, heartbroken
Out of life.
They were all Mexican and
It was in Mexico.
So I stayed out of it.
Did you ever see a boxer take a nap
In the middle of his opponent's pounding?
Just say Fuck it, I'm going to sleep.
Sure. A beaten man becomes elderly
And senile in an instant, dreaming
Of a moment, staring at a time from
Before he knew the fact of pain.
We kill ourselves first,
Then let ourselves be killed.
When I say ourselves I mean
They. They. They. Them. Maybe you,
You, probably.
Not me.
I have learned to fuse with assault,

With the unrefined, knuckleheaded
Hate, looking to succeed into the safety
Of sadism.
Like those niggers that danced
Around Reginald Denny.
Had I known he'd forgive them
On the Phil Donahue show
I would have gone there myself
And finished him off.
By hand.
And then just stood there
For the eyes in the sky to witness
Me fight.
I have paid the gooks for their
Family secrets and kicked them
In the face to capture
What they held back.
I have fought for knowledge
Of fighting and fucked
For the same.
You can develop a taste
And keep a fever maintained
Like a breed of dog
Cultivated to thrive on rabies.
I swear by all
I hold sacred.
Bruce Lee, Elvis, John Keats,
And Custer.
I will put my right arm up
And into a completely damned
Nazi salute to the God of that
First tough half of the Bible
And swear to Him who doesn't

Give a damn for me or Adam and Eve
That I would have simply liked
To sit and read all my life.
In this world I never made
In this fight I never started
And can't and won't stop
I was sitting and reading
On the subway train, a Sunday morning,
Six forty-five A.M.
I was going to work,
Sitting there alone, the car to myself,
Sitting and reading letters from
John Keats to that bitch who didn't
Give him any,
When three men invaded
At Fourteenth Street.
It felt like I flew down
Then tore upward
Like the jolt of a parachute
Hooked way behind me in the sky.
I was awarded ears
In an empty Coliseum
And tossed them down the car.
I was called a motherfucker
As I reached into another man's
Eyes.
I thought of Oedipus at his suggestion
And I felt confirmed
By the coincidence.
Man number three fled the car.
We were in the second car of the train.
He opened the doors between the cars.
He slammed them behind him.

He held the second door shut.
He was alone in the empty
First car of the train
Pressing all of himself on the handle
Of the door of the train
That stopped at Eighth Street
Where I ran to join him.
In that empty first car
That we filled up with pain,
Mine roaring, his howling,
As we followed the directions
I have discovered
And tattooed down my arm.
Fill
To
Bursting.
And
The Viking symbol
For Eternity.

On a Postcard of a Boxer That I Sent to Michael

You can run
But you can't hide
Joe Louis told Billy Conn
And one man will tell that
To another
After we're long gone

So don't kid yourself
And don't kid me
Men live to live out themes
Play the part you know by heart
And disconnect
Bad dreams.

Also Known As

This book has two titles.
Both I got in the exact same way
from stories people told me about these two men.
Albert Einstein and Sonny Liston.
The smartest guy who ever lived
and the toughest guy who ever lived.
The Nobel Prize for Physics
and the Heavyweight Champion of the World.
They gave me the official title
and the secret title.
The official title is on the cover.
Everything So Seriously.
That comes from Albert
saying that while he did not know
what would happen after he died
he did know that his first thought
would be: Why did I take
everything so seriously?
And the secret title
comes from Sonny.
Nobody Give Me No Breakfast.
Which I was told was his reply
to the Black Panthers
who rang the bell of his home
in Vegas one morning
to ask if he would
make a contribution
to their breakfast program
for schoolkids.
Sonny thought about it
for a minute.
He was in his robe
looking much like he did

in the ring
when he would listen to the ref's
instructions as if they came
from too far away to be paid
any mind to.
Just part of this world's wishful thinking.
That means nothing
where the first language
is not language.
Sonny Liston then spoke
this book's secret title
and with one finger
detonated the slam of his
door.
I had to tinker hard to make it
qualify.
Like hammering steel toward
sculpture
to find the light that's poetry
in his words.
Though it shone through a
pinhole
it was there. As a plea of
explanation for the achievement
of his hardness.
Hunger taught how Sonny fought.
Here is his poem, like a warning to the world.
Nobody
Give Me
No
Breakfast.

I dream them together.
Together they meld

into the perfect one.
I place Albert on Sonny's shoulders
and have them hike the universe.
Albert whiter than white
silver as starlight
and Sonny blacker than black
like a chunk cut from the night.
Following a map of calculations
they troop themselves
beyond this galaxy
and all the nexts
to the very lip of the wall
that ends space itself
where Albert will locate the
spot to place his finger
for Sonny to see
and nod at, once.
Before he punches it.
Then God will say something
that God has never said before.
"What
The Fuck
Was
That?"
And in the dream I say:
That was everything, my Lord.
And I say it
so seriously.

Douglas Treem lives and works in New York City.

About NYQ Books™

NYQ Books™ was established in 2009 as an imprint of The New York Quarterly Foundation, Inc. Its mission is to augment the *New York Quarterly* poetry magazine by providing an additional venue for poets already published in the magazine. A lifelong dream of NYQ's founding editor, William Packard, NYQ Books™ has been made possible by both growing foundation support and new technology that was not available during William Packard's lifetime. We are proud to present these books to you and hope that you will continue to support The New York Quarterly Foundation, Inc. and our poets and that you will enjoy these other titles from NYQ Books™:

Barbara Blatner	*The Still Position*
Amanda J. Bradley	*Hints and Allegations*
rd coleman	*beach tracks*
Joanna Crispi	*Soldier in the Grass*
Ira Joe Fisher	*Songs from an Earlier Century*
Sanford Fraser	*Tourist*
Tony Gloeggler	*The Last Lie*
Ted Jonathan	*Bones & Jokes*
Richard Kostelanetz	*Recircuits*
Iris Lee	*Urban Bird Life*
Kevin Pilkington	*In the Eyes of a Dog*
Jim Reese	*ghost on 3rd*
F. D. Reeve	*The Puzzle Master and Other Poems*
Jackie Sheeler	*Earthquake Came to Harlem*
Jayne Lyn Stahl	*Riding with Destiny*
Shelley Stenhouse	*Impunity*
Tim Suermondt	*Just Beautiful*
Douglas Treem	*Everything So Seriously*
Oren Wagner	*Voluptuous Gloom*
Joe Weil	*The Plumber's Apprentice*
Pui Ying Wong	*Yellow Plum Season*
Fred Yannantuono	*A Boilermaker for the Lady*
Grace Zabriskie	*Poems*

Please visit our website for these and other titles:

www.nyqbooks.org

Breinigsville, PA USA
18 December 2010
251728BV00003B/1/P